THE CHANGING FACE OF
AMERICA

PETER C. JONES

PRENTICE
HALL
PRESS

New York London Toronto Sydney Tokyo Singapore

Prentice Hall Press
15 Columbus Circle
New York, New York 10023

PRENTICE HALL PRESS and colophon are registered trademarks of Simon & Schuster, Inc.

Library of Congress Cataloging-in-Publication Data

Jones, Peter C.
    The changing face of America / by Peter C. Jones.
        p.   cm.
    Includes index.
    ISBN 0-13-028630-3
    1. Photography—Landscapes—Exhibitions.
    2. United States—Description and travel—Views—
Exhibitions. I. Title.
TR660.J66   1991
779'.3673'0973—dc20   90-28684
                                        CIP

Manufactured in the United States of America

10 9 8 7 6 5 4 3 2 1

First Edition

We have endeavored to provide necessary permission to reprint the photographs in this volume and to provide proper credit. We welcome information on any oversight which will be corrected in subsequent editions.

Opposite. MAID OF THE MIST, NIAGARA FALLS, 1915 (photograph by Paul Strand, courtesy Galerie Zur Stockeregg, Zurich, © 1982 Aperture Foundation, Inc., Paul Strand Archive)

Page 1. CONTOUR PLOWING, Colorado, 1954 (photograph by Margaret Bourke-White, *Life* magazine, © 1954 Time Warner, Inc.)

Pages 2 and 3. PANORAMA OF SAN FRANCISCO FROM CALIFORNIA STREET HILL, 1878, shot from the roof of the Mark Hopkins mansion at the top of Nob Hill (photographs by Eadweard Muybridge, courtesy Sotheby's), rephotographed by Mark Klett in 1990 from the sixteenth floor of the Mark Hopkins Hotel, site of the former Mark Hopkins mansion from ONE CITY / TWO VISIONS: SAN FRANCISCO PANORAMAS, 1878 AND 1990, an accordion fold of both panoramas published by Bedford Arts Publishers, 1990 (reprinted with the permission of Bedford Arts Publishers, San Francisco); the Mark Klett panorama was originally published in portfolio form by Fraenkel Gallery (courtesy Fraenkel Gallery, San Francisco)

Page 4. CANYON DE CHELLE, 1904 (photograph by Edward S. Curtis, courtesy Galerie Zur Stockeregg, Zurich)

Page 9. ARROYO, NEW MEXICO, 1930 (photograph by Paul Strand, courtesy Galerie Zur Stockeregg, Zurich, © 1981 Aperture Foundation, Inc., Paul Strand Archive)

Page 11. MIDWESTERN LANDSCAPE NUMBER 36, 1961 (photograph by Art Sinsabaugh, courtesy Indiana University Art Museum)

CONTENTS

CHAPTER

1

OPEN SPACES

In New England, a particular fragrance rises from the ground as the early July sun heats the fields still moist from the spring rains. A faint cloud of moisture hovers over the land, carrying with it the fertile aroma of newly grown grasses and wildflowers still in bloom. A screen door slams in the distance. Summer has begun.

The pleasures of open space come easily to mind: huge skies, clean air, the freedom to see great distances, a landscape defined by the sun. Still, the essence of open land is difficult to define. Photographer Robert Adams says simply, "The longer one is in a landscape, especially a spare one, the more one is likely to love it." However, Harvard professor John Stilgoe has concluded, "Whatever else the New England rural landscape is, it is for sale."

In 1980 the President's Council on Environmental Quality calculated that the amount of land being converted annually from open space to urban and suburban use could be stretched in a mile-wide strip extending from coast to coast. And the pace continues to accelerate.

Once all of America's lands were open, devoid of structures. No one had to seek out remote places. Now one sees pavement everywhere, even in the desert, where the intrusion of man is particularly poignant. The impact of just one building in an open landscape will shatter its fragile beauty.

Albert F. Appleton of the Audubon Society developed a rough formula for calculating the impact of development on open space: "The first 5 percent of development in a countryside region generally does about 50 percent of the damage in altering people's mental geography of an area. The second 5 percent enlarges this damage by another 50 percent."

The quality of America's remaining open space is under assault from all quarters. In 1985 the air force proposed to appropriate a six-hundred-acre hilltop potato field located on the Ashfield and Hawley town line in the Berkshire Hills in western Massachusetts and to litter the horizon with a thirty-one-antenna telecommunications facility. To complete the spectacle, each of the 240-foot towers would be lighted at night.

The air force's strategy to divide and conquer the two local communities ran into tactical difficulties with the farmers, who pointed out that the loss of the land would reduce what was left of the state's potato fields by 10 percent. Armed with the 1982 *Massachusetts Landscape Inventory,* which had designated the area a central feature of a "distinctive" landscape, local politicians quickly lined up against the project. The *Boston Globe* dubbed it an antenna farm. Ultimately, after several months of intense pressure, the air force capitulated.

The weather, too, is a culprit. In 1990 Illinois's worst tornado in twenty years dropped without warning from the heavy August sky, churning an eight-mile course of disaster through the cornfields and subdivisions of Will County, about thirty-five miles southwest of Chicago. Twenty-five people were killed, some literally sucked into the sky, their bodies found in the mashed cornfields. Three hundred fifty were injured as crumpled cars and shattered homes were tossed like wheat in the wind. Trees were reduced to splinters, and those left standing were stripped of their leaves, their branches shrouded with chunks of metal and shreds of clothing.

Despite these hazards, more than half of all Americans claim that they would prefer life in a rural setting, on a farm or in a small town, to that of a metropolitan center. But actions speak louder than words. From 1950 to 1990 the metropolitan

ANCIENT RUINS IN THE CANYON DE CHELLE, NEW MEXICO, 1873 (photograph by Timothy O'Sullivan, courtesy The J. Paul Getty Museum, albumen print, 10⅞" × 9⁹/₁₆")

Opposite. HEAD OF CANYON DE CHELLE LOOKING DOWN, 1873 (photograph by Timothy O'Sullivan, courtesy The J. Paul Getty Museum, albumen print, 10⅞" × 9⁹/₁₆")

centers, particularly in the suburbs, have enjoyed vast expansion while the rural population has diminished from 44 percent to 23 percent. Small towns have shriveled, reduced solely to mythological status as the quintessential American hometown.

Iowa has suffered the steepest decline of any state, with more than 5 percent of its population leaving in just ten years. In 1990 a poster in the town of Jefferson promised a one-thousand-dollar reward to anyone who could attract a business that would provide at least fifteen jobs. Scranton, Iowa, was way past finder's fees. The town's arcade, even its drugstore, was a distant memory. The high school closed in 1987. The remaining students went about ten miles east to Jefferson, but failed to bolster its enrollment, which dropped by half in the 1980s.

While a home on the range became a cherished myth, a home in the desert among the sand, sagebrush, and Joshua trees has become a cherished reality. During the 1980s California's desert oasis, Palm Springs, enjoyed great growth, but recent prosperity does not reflect its rugged beginnings, when settlers struggled to survive in the beautiful but forbidding open landscape.

The resource of water was certainly the magnet for the creation of Palm Springs, which was undiscovered until 1823, when Captain José Romero, who was looking for the Colorado River, paused at the natural hot springs and took a bath. An 1851 railroad survey gave a detailed description of the palm-shaded mineral pool and surrounding hot springs. Pony Express riders were the first to take advantage of this news. Soon a stage stop became a town.

However, in 1893 Palm Springs suffered a twenty-one-day downpour that washed out the crops and irrigation ditches. The rain was followed by an eleven-year

PROFILE HOUSE AND ECHO LAKE, FRANCONIA NOTCH, WHITE MOUNTAINS, NEW HAMPSHIRE, 1883 (photograph by David W. Butterfield, courtesy The J. Paul Getty Museum, albumen print, 17⅜" x 21¹¹/₁₆")

drought that forced settlers to drink highly sulfuric water from the mineral springs. Most of the town's inhabitants went bankrupt and moved away.

The Desert Inn was opened in 1909 as a sanatorium. Word of this wonderful refuge spread quickly, and a new brochure was published specifying "no invalids," to exclude the possibility of communicable disease from those coming to sample the mineral springs. By 1926 The Desert Inn had become a world renowned resort.

Located an hour and a half from Los Angeles by car, the oasis soon attracted Hollywood celebrities, and Palm Springs became unique among cities by naming streets after living people. For almost seven decades Palm Springs has developed exponentially. Water for lawns and golf courses has produced the greening of the desert, but it has also dramatically raised the level of humidity, creating a special kind of smog. As Palm Springs looks to the twenty-first century with water in short supply, it may have to choose between providing water for its citizens and water for its lawns.

Early developers of the prairie actually argued that settlement would increase rainfall. In Texas investors used open land to make money in oil and cattle and by persuading legislators to build highways through recently acquired open land. The investors then leased the land along the highway to stores and towns that would spring up like magic.

The rich man's view of open land is the golf course. However, an afternoon spent on a sliver of green belt, insulated from the cares of daily metropolitan life, is at best an imitation of the vast open space that once comprised America. For Americans, open space has always seemed available, there just for the taking. Only recently has it become widely understood that the supply is finite.

Horsemen gallop alongside Teddy Roosevelt's presidential train in Idaho, circa 1903 (courtesy Keystone Mast Collection, California Museum of Photography, University of California, Riverside)

Opposite. SANTO DOMINGO, NEW MEXICO, circa 1875 (photograph by John K. Hillers, courtesy The J. Paul Getty Museum, platinum print, 9⅝" x 12⁷/₁₆")

SANTO DOMINGO NM

Opposite. MONUMENT VALLEY, 1979 (photograph by Joan Myers, courtesy Linda Durham Gallery, Santa Fe)

Pages 22 and 23. Train trestle under construction, Cheyenne, Wyoming, 1905 (photograph by J. E. Stimson, courtesy Union Pacific Railroad)

Page 24. UBEHEBE CRATER AREA, DEATH VALLEY, 1938 (photograph by Edward Weston, courtesy Center for Creative Photography, © 1981 Arizona Board of Regents)

Page 25. HOT COFFEE, Mojave Desert, 1937 (photograph by Edward Weston, courtesy Center for Creative Photography, © 1981 Arizona Board of Regents)

Page 28. PRAIRIE GRASSES AND TELEPHONE WIRES, Lincoln County, Colorado, 1977 (photograph by Robert Adams, courtesy Fraenkel Gallery, San Francisco)

Page 29. An alkaline pool in the distance in Albany County, Wyoming, 1978 (photograph by Robert Adams, courtesy Fraenkel Gallery, San Francisco)

Opposite. LANDSCAPE NUMBER 2, NEW MEXICO, 1978 (photograph by William Clift)

Page 30. DESERT FORM NUMBER 3, NEW MEXICO, 1984 (photograph by William Clift)

Page 31. DESERT FORM NUMBER 2, NEW MEXICO, 1985 (photograph by William Clift)

Pages 34 and 35. AROUND TOROWEAP POINT, Grand Canyon, Arizona, 1986 (photograph by Mark Klett, courtesy Fraenkel Gallery, San Francisco, and Pace/MacGill Gallery, New York)

2

NATURAL WONDERS

The artist sketching at the Delaware Water Gap is believed to be the painter Thomas Moran (photograph by John Moran, 1864, courtesy The Robert N. Dennis Collection of Stereoscopic Views, Miriam and Ira D. Wallach Division of Art, Prints & Photographs, The New York Public Library Astor, Lenox and Tilden Foundations)

America's monumental natural beauty defies description, and since the invention of the camera, photographers have sought the challenge of distilling the essence of our magnificent wilderness landscape. Entranced by beauty on a vast scale against a backdrop of incredible natural forces, landscape photographers have created exquisite pictures by capturing natural light at the moment it defines the landscape.

Photographers are deeply concerned with context. What is excluded from a photograph can be just as important as what is included. But for landscape photographers, the journey into the wilderness can be a critical influence on the ultimate composition, often establishing the content of a picture even before the tripod is set up.

Ansel Adams once described climbing the long ridge west of Mount Clark in California's Sierra Nevada range: "It was one of those mornings when the sunlight is burnished with a keen wind and long feathers of clouds move in a lofty sky.

Page 37. TASAYAC, HALF DOME FROM GLACIER POINT, Yosemite, circa 1865 (photograph by Carlton Emmons Watkins, from The Quillan Collection, courtesy Jill Quasha, New York)

The silver light turned every blade of grass and every particle of sand into a luminous metallic splendor. . . . I was suddenly arrested in the long . . . path up the ridge by an exceedingly pointed awareness of light. . . . I saw more clearly than I have ever seen before or since the minute detail of grasses . . . the motion of the high clouds streaming above the peaks. There are no words to convey the moods of those moments."

Edward Weston wrote in his daybook about his experiences the day of March 1, 1929, "I started my work again!—and in the most exciting of environs—the Big Sur. . . . The excursion was exciting, over a steep tortuous road high upon the cliffs overlooking the Pacific, then down into valleys . . . where great Redwoods, majestically silent, towered toward the light. The coast was on a grand scale: mountainous cliffs thrust buttresses far out into the ocean, anchored safely for an eternity: against the rising sun, their black solidity accentuated by rising mists, and sunlit water." But for Weston, as for all photographers, it is the pictures that count. He continued, "I lack words [for] I am inarticulate, [and] anything I might write would sound as trivial as 'ain't nature grand.' "

Awe is the common bond felt by all who look upon the abyss of America's great natural wonders. The first man to drive a car to the edge of the Grand Canyon uttered the now universal sentiment: "I stood there upon the rim of that tremendous chasm and forgot who I was and what I came there for." Ansel Adams wrote his wife, Virginia, in the 1930s that "Canyon de Chelly exceeds anything I have imagined at any time."

While many photographers have concentrated on grand views of the landscape, contemporary photographer Lois Conner is passionate about trees. "I feel like my pictures of trees are portraits," she said in describing her platinum prints made with an old seven-by-seventeen-inch banquet camera that has been reinforced with parts handcrafted by her father. "I may see a limb in the distance and walk miles to photograph the tree. Sometimes the light on a branch just calls out. Sometimes my response is immediate. You may walk past a certain tree one hundred times and not notice it until the one hundred and first encounter when it is enshrouded in fog. Suddenly, the light may come out of the clouds and never be like that again."

Before the Civil War, the federal government began to commission photographic surveys of the western states, initially to identify railroad routes, later to gather military reconnaissance for the forthcoming war with the southwestern Indians, and ultimately to form an assessment of the region's economic potential. Unlike their European counterparts, American photographers did not have the luxury of porters to tote their equipment. Instead special vans were constructed. However, when the terrain became impassable to vehicles, photographers had to resort to pack animals to haul their gear.

Then as now, location photography requires constant unpacking and repacking. In addition to cameras, lenses, and tripods, photographers carried glass plates of various sizes and an array of chemicals. The preparation and processing of the plates was often hampered by the lack of pure water. The sticky collodion emulsion used by the photographers attracted dust and bugs. Unsuccessful pictures were scraped off the plates so the glass could be recoated for another try. Early photographic emulsions had an extreme sensitivity to blue and consequently rendered the sky white. To add drama, photographers often superimposed clouds from another negative onto the final print.

CAPTAINS OF THE CANYON, CANYON DE CHELLE, ARIZONA, 1870s (photograph by John K. Hillers, courtesy The J. Paul Getty Museum, albumen print, 13⁵/₃₂" x 9 ³¹/₃₂")

Opposite. GRAND CANYON, COLORADO RIVER, ARIZONA, circa 1875 (photograph by John K. Hillers, The J. Paul Getty Museum, albumen print, 13⁷/₃₂" x 9¹⁵/₁₆")

GRAND CAÑON COLORADO RIVER ARIZ

An exception was Timothy O'Sullivan, perhaps America's greatest landscape photographer, who accepted the confines of the medium and produced spare, elegant compositions that captured the essence of the open land around him. During the Civil War, O'Sullivan transported his equipment in a horse-drawn ambulance. The appalling conditions he found on the battlefield may have prepared him for his journeys farther west on the government explorations of the 40th parallel and the 100th meridian from 1867 to 1874. Work and, ultimately, survival meant traveling immense distances in uncertain directions while encountering extreme heat and cold, swarms of voracious mosquitoes, and hostile Indians. Proceeding by water was also hazardous, and during the 1871 expedition several of the boats capsized in the Colorado River and approximately three hundred of O'Sullivan's negatives were destroyed.

Other photographers suffered similar fates. Nearly blind at the end of his life, the brilliant landscape photographer Carlton Watkins was dragged from the smoldering ruin of his San Francisco studio after the great earthquake of 1906 and watched as much of his life's work burst into flames. Edward Weston once helped Ansel Adams extinguish his darkroom fire, but not before approximately five thousand negatives of Yosemite were destroyed.

Fundamentally a populist medium, unsurpassed in its poignancy, photography has made Americans aware of their natural treasures. These photographs require no explanation, and some would say they have vastly diminished the importance of western landscape paintings.

The majesty of purple mountains really does exist.

LEAPING THE CHASM AT STAND ROCK, Wisconsin Dells, 1886 (photograph by H. H. Bennett, courtesy H. H. Bennett Studio Foundation)

Opposite. GLACIER POINT, 3,201 FEET, YOSEMITE VALLEY, CALIFORNIA, 1887 (photographer unknown, courtesy Daniel Wolte, Inc., New York)

MIRROR VIEW OF EL CAPITAN, YO SEMITE VALLEY, circa 1864 (photograph by Charles Leaner Weed, courtesy The J. Paul Getty Museum, albumen print, 20⅜ × 15⅝)

Opposite. YOSEMITE VALLEY NO. 1, 1865–66 (photograph by Carlton Emmons Watkins, courtesy Fraenkel Gallery, San Francisco)

YO-SEM-I-TE VALLEY CALIFORNIA: SUMMIT OF THE
LOWER YO-SEM-I-TE FALL AT LOW WATER, circa 1870
(photograph by Edweard Muybridge, courtesy
The J. Paul Getty Museum, albumen print, 7⅞ ×
5⅞)

Opposite. AGASSIZ COLUMN, NEAR UNION POINT,
circa 1870 (photograph attributed to Carlton
Emmons Watkins, courtesy Sotheby's)

President Theodore Roosevelt standing on Glacier Point at Yosemite, 1903 (courtesy Keystone Mast Collection, California Museum of Photography, University of California, Riverside)

Opposite. The "Old Faithful" geyser in Yellowstone National Park rises to the occasion around the turn of the century (courtesy Lisa S. Adelson Collection)

Opposite. FACTORY BUTTE, UTAH, 1975 (photograph by William Clift)

Pages 50 and 51. Larch oaks at Bon Aventure
Cemetery, Mulryne County, Georgia, circa 1870
(photograph by J. N. Wilson, courtesy The Robert N. Dennis Collection of Stereoscopic Views,
Miriam and Ira D. Wallach Division of Art, Prints
& Photographs, The New York Public Library Astor, Lenox and Tilden Foundations)

Page 52. CYPRESS, POINT LOBOS, 1944 (photo-
graph by Edward Weston, courtesy Center for
Creative Photography, © 1981 Arizona Board of
Regents)

Page 53. WHITE HOUSE RUIN, CANYON DE CHELLE,
ARIZONA, 1975 (photograph by William Clift)

Between one and one hundred feet of pulverized ash covered MT. ST. HELENS, WASHINGTON, in 1984, following the aftermath of the 1980 eruption (photograph by Emmet Gowin, courtesy Pace/MacGill Gallery, New York)

Opposite. AERIAL VIEW: MT. ST. HELENS CRATER AND LAVA DOME, AIRPLANE IN CRATER, MTS. HOOD & JEFFERSON IN THE DISTANCE, 1982 (photograph by Frank Gohlke, courtesy Franklin Parrasch Gallery, New York, and Bonnie Benrubi Fine Arts, New York)

Entering a narrow cave.   Salt Creek 5/9/90

ENTERING A NARROW CAVE, SALT CREEK, Utah, May 4, 1990 (photograph by Mark Klett, courtesy Fraenkel Gallery, San Francisco, and Pace/MacGill Gallery, New York)

Opposite. BEEHIVE GEYSER, YELLOWSTONE NATIONAL PARK, WYOMING, 1990 (photograph by Lynn Davis, courtesy Hirschl & Adler Modern, New York)

CHAPTER

3

RIVERS

For millions of years the Colorado River has wound its 1,400-mile course from the Rocky Mountains to the Gulf of California. Historically regarded as a wellspring of destruction, it flowed for decades in a boom or bust cycle that complemented the spirit of the early western development. Swollen each year by melting spring snows, the river overflowed its banks with a torrent of water, destroying crops and property and taking lives. In late summer the river regularly ran dry and utterly defeated early efforts at irrigation. Without water, crops and livestock withered and died.

Catastrophe occurred in 1905, when a diversion of Colorado River water to California's Imperial Valley for irrigation was overwhelmed by a combination of early-spring flash floods and an abnormally high spring runoff. As the enormous volume of water crushed the small earthen dams, cutting a deep channel in the Imperial Canal, the river changed course and flooded the valley. And the river continued flooding the Imperial Valley for more than sixteen months before resuming its original course.

Engineers, including Herbert Hoover, who became president of the United States in 1929, set out to turn this mighty river into a reliable source of water, irrigation, and hydroelectric power for the thirsty developing western cities and farmlands. It took until 1922 to reach an agreement apportioning the use of the Colorado's water; Congress took another six years to authorize construction of Hoover Dam.

Completed in 1935, two years ahead of schedule, Hoover Dam stands as one of the wonders of the modern world and the pivotal element in the development of southern California and the western United States. As the Colorado River was retained behind the dam, a reservoir known as Lake Mead was created. This reservoir, which is 110 miles long when full and stretches into the lower end of the

Grand Canyon, irrigates some of America's richest farmland. Almost two-thirds of the hydroelectricity generated is distributed to southern California. By regulating the Colorado River, Hoover Dam assures a steady flow of municipal and industrial water to Los Angeles, San Diego, Las Vegas, and Phoenix.

Like all successes, Hoover Dam was imitated. Hydroelectric dams check the flow of small rivers throughout the nation, creating inexpensive electricity, but often at substantial ecological cost. One plant keeps the lights burning for only 1,800 privileged customers, while another, used exclusively to provide power to a pulp plant, prevents the breeding of the giant hundred-pound chinook salmon. Unlike these limited-purpose dams, Hoover Dam was a visionary project, undertaken to maximize ancillary benefits for the nation.

As much as America has tamed its powerful rivers with dams and levees, these ribbons of water have not capitulated. Notwithstanding the Army Corps of Engineers' massive construction of levees along the banks of the Mississippi River to improve navigation, America's largest river and central waterway ran dry in the late 1980s, causing havoc as boats ran aground on its soft bottom. Despite efforts at diverting the runoff, many rivers still overflow their banks during the spring thaw. Televised images of car roofs poking through flooded streets while residents paddle skiffs past second-floor windows are as much a sign of the season as spring training.

The life of a river flows in cycles. Shortly after the Civil War the Hudson River, named for the explorer Henry Hudson, was renowned for its pastoral beauty and dramatic cloud formations. Artists flocked to its banks. Although valued as a major transportation artery, by the turn of the century, as industrialization spread up river, the Hudson and its environs became fouled by the black smoke belching from factory smokestacks.

Placid waters, soon polluted by industrial waste, became unfit to swim in. But the economy was finally to intervene, and demand for Hudson River industrial products dropped. Factories became idle and were ultimately abandoned, and after a long and hard battle pollution was brought under control.

Today, many factory buildings along the Hudson River have been renovated into retail shops and offices. Others have become ruins—a traditional accent in the now revitalized pastoral landscape. Paintings from the Hudson River School have never been more popular, and although the striped bass continue to be contaminated by thirty years of PCB dumping by the General Electric Company, the fishing above Albany, New York, is considered pretty good.

Americans have never been afraid to contaminate their own water supply, but, with the specter of pollution, attitudes have changed. While the great engineering victories of the past were a clear benefit to the nation, the bounty they unleashed allowed for the misuse and waste of precious resources.

It is hard to imagine a time when the waters around urban and industrial centers ran free and clear. For proof that they did, one must look to historical documents such as the advertisement that ran in an 1871 New York newspaper announcing that a three-hundred-pound green turtle had been caught in the East River and would be eaten at Joseph's restaurant at 1:00 P.M. on Thursday. Such a feast would be inconceivable today.

DOWN RIVER FROM GRAND AVENUE BRIDGE, Milwaukee, Wisconsin, circa 1880 (photograph by H. H. Bennett, courtesy H. H. Bennett Studio Foundation)

Opposite. CAPE HORN, COLUMBIA RIVER, Oregon, 1867 (photograph by Carlton Emmons Watkins, courtesy Fraenkel Gallery, San Francisco)

Dynamite was used in CLEARING THE CHANNEL, Cascade Rapids, Columbia River, Oregon, 1882 (photograph by Carlton Emmons Watkins, courtesy Oregon Historical Society, negative ORHI 70247)

Opposite. THE PASSAGE OF THE DALES, Columbia River, Oregon, 1882 (photograph by Carlton Emmons Watkins, courtesy Oregon Historical Society, negative ORHI 21649)

LOOKING INTO BOAT CAVE, Upper Dells of the Wisconsin River, circa 1880 (photograph by H. H. Bennett, courtesy H. H. Bennett Studio Foundation).

Opposite. MECHANICS ROCK, Mississippi River, circa 1888 (photograph by Henry Bosse under the direction of Major Alexander Mackenzie, courtesy Sotheby's)

Pages 72 and 73. NIAGARA FALLS, January 1885 (photograph by H. F. Neilson & Co., courtesy The J. Paul Getty Museum, detail of an albumen print, 15⁹/₁₆″ x 18⁹/₁₆″)

Opposite. THE LAD, BEAR MOUNTAIN BRIDGE, HUD-
SON RIVER, 1986 (photograph by William Clift)

Page 74. Site for Hoover Dam at Black Canyon
on the Colorado River, 1922 (photograph by
W. R. Young, courtesy Bureau of Reclamation)

Page 75. Hoover Dam, which spans the Colorado River between Nevada and Arizona, was
completed in 1935—two years ahead of schedule—
and remains one of the most successful engineering projects in American history (photograph by
Eugene E. Hertzog, courtesy Bureau of Reclamation)

Pages 76 and 77. CONFLUENCE OF THE COLORADO
AND GREEN RIVERS, Utah, 1972 (photograph by
David Avison)

Only 11 percent of the world's surface is rich, productive farmland, and a very large portion of that land is embraced by the boundaries of the continental United States. At the time of the Declaration of Independence, America was an agrarian society, a nation of farmers, a land of working landscapes. Much of this farmland has been transformed into the urban and suburban landscapes prevalent today, paved with highways and covered with residential subdivisions, malls, and long commercial strips. What land remains is precious.

In 1929 Massachusetts was more than 40 percent farmland, but by 1980 its agricultural landscape had shrunk to only 10 percent. New York State lost close to a million acres of farmland between 1982 and 1987. To preserve open farmland as a working landscape, the government has been purchasing farming development rights—the difference between the land's value to a farmer and to a developer—and will hold the rights in perpetuity.

The owners of family farms, such as New York State's seven-generation Lain farm, have set up living trusts to keep the property intact. Although dairy farming has been forsaken for wheat, wool, and Holsteins, descendents of William Lain continue to live in his original 1785 stone farmhouse and are in the agricultural vanguard in their use of organic farming techniques.

However, not all farms that vanish are lost to developers. Throughout New England, much of the working landscape that now lies fallow after more than a hundred years of farming has returned to woodlands, and in an American version of the English garden ruin, second-growth forests are dotted with abandoned foundations and crossed by aesthetically pleasing stone walls whose original function has long since passed.

THE DUST STORM, CIMARRON, OKLAHOMA, 1936 (photograph by Arthur Rothstein, courtesy Library of Congress)

Page 80. MIDWESTERN LANDSCAPE NUMBER 60, 1961 (photograph by Art Sinsabaugh, courtesy Indiana University Art Museum)

Page 81. TRACTORED OUT, CHILDRESS COUNTY, TEXAS, 1938 (photograph by Dorothea Lange, courtesy Houk Friedman Gallery, New York)

Historically, farms have been the playing fields of war. During the Civil War the decisive battle of Antietam was fought largely on the prosperous Miller, Piper, and Roulette farms, which became the setting for battle smoke and roar, cannon shot, and hissing bullets. While soldiers of both sides sought cover in the orchards and cornfields, a tense regiment of rookie Union troops awaited battle at the Roulette farm. A rebel sharpshooter, firing into the beehives, gave them more than bullets to worry about. Attacked by swarms of angry bees, the Union troops scattered in utter chaos. General Williams wrote, "If all the stone and brick houses of Broadway should tumble at once, the roar and rattle could hardly be greater . . . amidst . . . hundreds of pieces of artillery." After the battle an eerie quiet settled in. The thirty-acre Miller cornfield had been leveled as if cut down by a scythe. Officers established headquarters in the farmhouses, while the surgeons turned the Roulette barn into a field infirmary, assembling operating tables from barn planks and beds from straw.

Appalled by the sight of the bodies littering the farmlands, renowned portrait photographer Matthew Brady spent his fortune sending out teams of photographers to record the grisly spectacle. He believed that if people could see war as it is, all armed conflicts would cease. But after the Civil War no one wanted to see Brady's lantern slides, and he died penniless. However, with the televised forced feeding of the Vietnam War, Brady's belief that photography could stop a war was realized.

The military legacy of the cold war quietly persists for America's farmlands. In 1983 photographer Robert Adams wrote, "On grassland northeast of Denver the Rocky Mountain Arsenal has buried in shallow trenches, without record of location, wheat rust agent made originally for germ warfare; the dump is upwind of the

American wheat bowl and there is apparently nothing to prevent prairie dogs or a badger from someday opening it."

America's prairies have been known by different names: the Great Plains; America's bread basket; and, most poignantly, the dust bowl. The thick roots of the prairie grasses once spread as much as six feet deep and held in place magnificent topsoil, created over thousands of years. However, in the 1920s plows, pulled by tractors for the first time, could slice through the roots, which enabled massive plantings of wheat as a cash crop.

Cimarron County, Oklahoma, is at the heart of the Great Plains, which includes parts of Colorado, New Mexico, Nebraska, Kansas, Texas, and Oklahoma. In the early twenties, farmers flocked to the area, known as wheat heaven, from as far away as Chicago and the East Coast. Some came to live and farm, others were "suitcase farmers," urban professionals who came to plant and harvest while continuing their careers in between the seasons. Grassland cost about fifteen dollars an acre. By placing 25 percent down, a farmer could expect to plow twenty bushels of wheat per acre, sell them for a dollar each, and pay for the land in a single summer.

By 1930 more than 5 million acres of the Great Plains had been plowed and planted. With the summer rains of 1931 the output rose from twenty to fifty bushels an acre. But ripples from the 1929 Wall Street crash overwhelmed the Great Plains like a tidal wave. The price of wheat collapsed, tumbling from a dollar to twenty-five cents a bushel. Drought began in 1932, and the wheat crop failed. Suitcase farmers packed up and abandoned their land, leaving behind vast acreages of plowed but unplanted fields. With no roots to hold the earth, all that magnificent topsoil simply blew away.

An army of harvesters marches across the plains, 1983 (courtesy The John Deere Company)

Opposite., TOMATO FIELD, BIG SUR (photograph by Edward Weston, 1937, courtesy The J. Paul Getty Museum, gelatin silver print, 7½″ x 9½″, © 1981 Arizona Board of Regents, Center for Creative Photography)

The morning of April 14, 1935, in Cimarron County was sunny and calm, yet another in a series of rainless days. In the afternoon a staggering dust storm blowing from the north came tearing over the horizon. The sun was completely obscured as it hit the towns of Kenton and Felt. The atmosphere was charged with electricity. Automobile ignitions burned out. Unable to see, people were lost a few hundred feet from their homes. When the storm cleared, their houses were buried, and Black Sunday was etched into their memories with all the pathos of an assassination.

The dark red-brown dust, soft as talcum powder, was everywhere—"in the beds and in the flour bin, on the dishes and walls and windows, in the hair and eyes and teeth and throats," wrote Oklahoma farmer Caroline Henderson in the *Atlantic Monthly*. Drifts in the attic went unnoticed until the ceiling caved in. By 1939 half of Oklahoma was on relief.

At the end of the decade the rains returned. The Great Plains became green again. Farmers who had stayed with their land began to repay their debts. But the 1950s brought a new drought, and the dust storms returned. As the topsoil blew away once again, the hardened tractor wheel prints from the mass plowing of the twenties resurfaced like dinosaur footprints of a more prosperous age.

America's farmland is the world's most magnificent working landscape and, perhaps, the nation's greatest natural resource. But the farmlands are disappearing at a rate that gives fresh meaning to the concept of depreciation. Ancillary consequences, such as the depletion and contamination of regional water supplies, are surfacing quickly. The end of America's once seemingly infinite bounty is in sight. The Great Plains can feed the world, but only if the nation acknowledges that its farmlands must be nurtured, not exploited.

Virginia tobacco harvest, shortly after the turn of the century (courtesy Valentine Museum, Richmond, Virginia)

Pages 88 and 89. 1908 saw the last roundup on the range as the XIT Cattle Company gathered a final herd near the forks of Burns Creek, about twenty miles north of Glendive, Montana (courtesy Montana Historical Society, Helena)

GRAIN ELEVATORS AND LIGHTNING FLASH, Lamesa, Texas, 1975 (photograph by Frank Gohlke, courtesy Franklin Parrasch Gallery, New York, and Bonnie Benrubi Fine Arts, New York)

CORNFIELD AND APPROACHING STORM, NEAR EARTH, TEXAS, 1975 (photograph by Frank Gohlke, courtesy Franklin Parrasch Gallery, New York, and Bonnie Benrubi Fine Arts, New York)

Page 92. CRACKED MUD AND VINEYARD, NEAR ARVIN, CALIFORNIA, 1985 (photograph by Robert Dawson)

Page 93. Washington State and northeast Oregon boast the deepest, richest topsoil in America, freshly plowed for planting at a farm near Pendleton, Oregon, 1978 (photograph by Robert Adams, courtesy Fraenkel Gallery, San Francisco)

5

SHORELINES

109 Palisades Mount... Love From Houghton's...

Opposite. PACIFIC COAST VIEW, 1870 (photograph by Carlton Emmons Watkins, courtesy The J. Paul Getty Museum, albumen print, 15 7/16" x 21 1/8")

Page 94. NANTUCKET, circa 1865 (photograph by J. Freeman, courtesy The Robert N. Dennis Collection of Stereoscopic Views, Miriam and Ira D. Wallach Division of Art, Prints & Photographs, The New York Public Library Astor, Lenox and Tilden Foundations)

Page 95. The Palisades Mountain View Hotel from Houghton's Point on the Hudson River, circa 1870 (photograph by Stoddard, courtesy Sachem Publishing Associates, Guilford, Connecticut)

Coastal swarms of unbridled growth shroud America's vast central landscape. The nation's beaches, once strips of tranquillity, have become battlegrounds for national priorities from oil exploration to waste disposal to real-estate development to public access and to the genesis of life, the tidal wetlands.

Shoreline erosion is constant, but nature, in its grand design, has always replenished the shorelines. However, contemporary demands for energy, commerce, and recreation have upset the natural balance and disrupted the shoreline's ability to renew itself. Only recently has the fragility and importance of the coastal ecosystems become widely understood.

The nation first perceived that its beaches were vulnerable on January 28, 1969, when, with a roar, the Union Oil Company's Well 21 on Oil Platform A off the coast of Santa Barbara blew up. Crewmen scrambled through showering mud to insert a seventy-five-pound check valve into the gaping mouth of the drill pipe, something like trying to screw a turbine into the mouth of a typhoon.

Pressure in the pipe hit 1,400 pounds per square inch. Suddenly, the mud shower stopped. A cloud of natural gas billowed up to the top of the rig. Afraid of explosion and fire, the crewmen abandoned the check valve and the mud pumps in favor of a last stand with the emergency sealing device called the "blind rams." They worked.

About fifteen minutes later the water began to bubble with gas, then came to a full boil. The sea surrounding Platform A raged as if in a steaming cauldron, with enormous boils spreading along the geological fault line on which the platform was constructed. By morning oil began leaking, then belching from the fissures in the seabed at a rate of 170,000 gallons a day. An oil slick more than an inch thick began heading for the beaches of southern California.

Within a week the oil slick covered two hundred square miles. As the slick began washing ashore south of Santa Barbara, Red Adair's oil-spill emergency crew arrived by helicopter and optimistically predicted rapid control of the situation.

Three days later they pumped 13,000 barrels of heavy mud into the well under enormous pressure, followed by more than a thousand sacks of cement. By midnight Well A-21 was capped and dead. Everyone relaxed. Cleanup could begin.

Eight hundred oil workers, supplemented by four hundred convicts, got to work. In an era of moon walks, straw was their chief cleanup weapon. Once dropped on the beach, it was quickly impregnated with oil, then picked up to be replaced with more straw. The oil-soaked straw was trucked to the local dump until it, too, began oozing oil, then on to Oxnard, and finally to Tajiquas, where some of the oil ultimately bled back into the sea.

A dead dolphin was found on the beach, its breathing hole plugged with oil. A spokesman for Governor Ronald Reagan's State Fish and Game Department disputed the conclusion that the dolphin had suffocated, saying, "We must have firm proof that these mammals are affected by oil, and that is difficult to determine."

After five days of bad weather scientists aboard the submersible observatory *Jordan* again discovered oil oozing out of the ocean floor at a rate of about three thousand gallons a day, creating a fresh surface slick extending as far as the eye could see. Red Adair and his crew had not completely corked the blowout.

President Nixon created the President's Panel on Oil Spills. Its chairman, John H. Calhoun, Jr., emerged from a closed session to say that the citizens of Santa Barbara were, in a sense, "guinea pigs" undergoing a traumatic experience for the ultimate benefit of the rest of American society.

LONG WHARF, Boston, circa 1880 (photograph by Augustine H. Folsom, courtesy The Boston Athenaeum)

A week later, despite loud local protests, President Nixon's panel ordered that all five wells on Platform A be pumped "at maximum rate" to relieve subterranean pressure. The leakage increased, and oil was washed ashore, blackening beaches as far as Catalina Island a hundred miles away. With the dumps full, Union Oil began setting fire to piles of oil-saturated straw on the beaches, soiling the sky with thick, oily smoke.

The best estimates indicate that 2.3 million gallons of oil were released into the Santa Barbara Channel during the first ten days after the blowout, with a further 950,000 gallons during the next ninety days. Fifty thousand more gallons of oil oozed from the fissures along the fault line over the next two years.

Shortly after the first anniversary of the spill, Richard Nixon had a change of heart. Describing the federal government as "one of the nation's worst polluters," he ordered all federal agencies to cease and desist and announced a $10 billion program "to bring pure water back to the people." He signed the Water Quality Act on April 3, 1970.

Not all ocean sludge is man made. Flecks of natural oil seepage found on beaches near Santa Barbara were once gathered by the Chumasa Indians for caulking their boats. In the summer of 1985 the Northeast endured its first impenetrable brown tide of Pico plankton, so thick that sunlight could not reach to the seabed.

The brown tide of Pico plankton first appeared in one of the most pristine estuaries in the Northeast, Great Peconic Bay, located between the two great forks at the western end of Long Island. Then it swept north across Narragansett Bay to Rhode Island and south to Barnegat Bay and New Jersey, rendering beaches unfit for swimming. Long Island's scallop beds were annihilated, as were most of the oysters. The brown tide returned in 1986 and 1987 and then, mysteriously, disappeared for two summers only to reappear in 1990, just as fishermen were contemplating the first limited harvest from the reseeded scallop beds. The cause of the brown tide has not yet been determined, and while numerous theories point to runoff and pollution, scientists believe natural forces may be the primary factors.

Storms play a great role in the romance of coastal lore. The skill of Maine fishermen comes to mind with images of a captain piloting his boat through the channel between the islands, battling twenty-five-foot waves and whistling winter winds, reaching safe harbor and then docking on a dime.

Hurricane Hugo made no romantic overtures toward Charleston in 1989. Jetties, built to keep sand in place, broke apart. Their boulders were tossed like pebbles, crushing homes five hundred feet away. Within hours new inlets were carved in the thin barrier islands, and barrier beaches were pushed back as much as one hundred fifty feet toward the mainland.

If such a major storm were to hit New York City, Kennedy Airport, under twenty-six feet of water, might look something like the New London submarine base, with the cockpits of 747s poking through the brine like conning towers. At Long Beach, New York, a barrier island off Long Island that is home to 35,000 people, a thirty-foot wall of water with cresting waves whipped by 140-mile-per-hour winds would demolish homes and apartment buildings. Further east another barrier island, the popular summer resort Fire Island, would be thrust more than a hundred feet toward mainland Long Island. At the George Washington Bridge the level of the Hudson River would rise at least twenty-eight feet above a full-moon high tide, flooding Manhattan and New Jersey.

SUGAR LOAF ISLANDS AND FISHERMAN'S BAY, FAR-ALLONS, 1869 (photograph by Carlton Emmons Watkins, courtesy The J. Paul Getty Museum, albumen print, 15^{13}/$_{16}$" x 20½")

After storms washed out fifteen miles of Miami's beaches in 1972, the city replaced the sand at a cost of $65 million to preserve its appeal as a tourist mecca. However, Hurricane Hugo has taught that erosion is part of the life cycle of a shoreline and that the replacement of Miami's beaches is unlikely to be permanent.

Poorly conceived erosion-control measures threaten the coastline's naturally fluid structure, while ongoing development limits public access. The spending of millions of dollars, often of public funds, to protect oceanfront development with jetties, seawalls, and sand-replenishment programs may be futile in repelling nature's relentless impulse to shove the barrier islands toward the mainland.

Like a dog pawing at a gopher hole, the ocean yearned to reach the calm waters behind Cape Cod's Nauset barrier beach at Chatham, Massachusetts. The corrosive ocean currents were intensified in 1958 when the Army Corps of Engineers constructed a roadway to gain access to then private Morris Island. As a major winter storm hit Chatham on January 1, 1987, waves crashed over the beach. By early morning the following day the beach was breached and the gap quickly widened to a hundred feet. Currents shifted radically, gnawing at the now exposed underbelly of the barrier beach, and sand began eroding along the adjacent coastline. Rip wrap walls were erected on the mainland to restrain erosion, aggravating the problem at neighboring properties. The hundred-foot breach has expanded to about a mile wide. On the mainland a hundred-foot portion of beach frontage, parking lot, and roadway has been bitten off, and five houses between Holway Street and Andrew Harding's Lane have been washed away.

Dramatic shoreline loss caused by storms is the underlying product of the gradual but constant erosion of protective dunes and beaches. Now accurately predicted

ATCHAFALAYA SWAMP, Louisiana, 1986 (photograph by Sally Gall, courtesy Lieberman & Saul Gallery, New York)

Opposite. UNTITLED LANDSCAPE, FLORIDA (photograph by George Barker, courtesy The J. Paul Getty Museum, albumen print, 16⅜″ x 20⁷⁄₁₆″)

by scientists, the inevitability of coastal erosion has motivated limitations for ocean-front development.

New home designs have also been inspired by erosion, such as those built on stilts that allow the wash of a major storm to pass beneath. When erosion persists, such structures, designed like a beachfront version of a mobile home, can be moved to new ground that has not been reclaimed by the sea.

New Jersey has undertaken an unusual approach to cleaning up the mounds of debris that litter its beaches by putting prison inmates to work hauling it away. Their prey, ranging from timbers to tar balls to pop tops and the odd satchel of medical waste, totaled 6.5 million pounds of trash in 1989, scoured from seventeen miles of shoreline.

In 1989 the New Jersey shoreline averaged 300,000 pounds of trash per mile, compared with the national average of 3,000 pounds of trash per mile. Much of the debris seems to come from crumbling docks and piers, remnants of once-thriving ports. Huge timbers, some as much as two feet square and twenty-five feet long, weighing as much as a station wagon, float downstream and wash ashore, perhaps at Bayonne, where they might lie for a month to a year or more, until with rising tides and heavy rains they float again, now bound, perhaps, for Perth Amboy.

The Department of Environmental Protection has undertaken the New Jersey Floatables Study to monitor all flotsam, from plastic cups to medical waste, and has initiated a "notes in the bottle" survey that has received excellent cooperation from the recipients of its missives.

Most of the bottles released in the Hudson or Raritan Bay come ashore on the northern coast of New Jersey. One bottle landed in Nantucket, another in Ber-

The great hurricane of 1938 first came ashore on eastern Long Island, then crossed Long Island Sound to pound New England; at least 600 people were killed, including 262 as the waves battered Rhode Island (courtesy THE PROVIDENCE JOURNAL Company, © 1991)

Galveston, Texas, in the aftermath of the 1900 hurricane that killed 6,000 people (courtesy Rosenberg Library, Galveston, Texas)

Page 106. A well-dressed crowd watches Jack McGee demonstrate his flying machine at Newport's Easton Beach in August 1912. Easton's Point in the distance was still almost entirely open land (© John T. Hoph, from *Newport Then & Now*)

Page 107. Hurricanes have twice demolished the beach buildings, and Easton's point is now crowded with houses (© John T. Hoph, from *Newport Then & Now*)

muda, another in the Azores, and in 1990 a bottle from northern New Jersey bumped ashore in Norway.

The 5 million acres of coastal wetlands that make up a quarter of Louisiana were once replenished by fresh water and sediment from the overflow of the Mississippi River. After the Army Corps of Engineers constructed levees along the river to prevent flooding and improve navigation, this incredibly rich ecosystem began to fill with salt water and is now eroding at the rate of an acre every fifteen minutes.

A daily torrent of 90,000 tons of once replenishing sediment now shoots uselessly out of the mouth of the Mississippi River into the deep waters off the continental shelf. In 1945, 91 percent of the Louisiana wetlands were stable, but by 1980, stable acreage had been reduced to only 28 percent. If nothing is done, St. Bernard Parish, an area the size of Delaware that is 90 percent wetlands, will be gone in a generation.

Almost half of America's wetlands have been irreversibly destroyed, and with them an increasing percentage of shellfish grounds are closed each year due to contamination, a direct result of the push and pull of entrenched interests. Compromise legislation does not acknowledge that all pollution is harmful and permits the release of pollution within limits acceptable to industry.

However, life is not a compromise, and life begins in the wetlands. A collective understanding of this essential ecosystem is crucial to the future of the nation. Ultimately, the impact from the way America treats its shorelines will reverberate throughout the planet.

UNTITLED NUMBER 1, FROM THE MONO LAKE SERIES,
1979 (photograph by Robert Dawson)

Top. Since 1941 water from Mono Lake has been drawn off for thirsty Los Angeles, and much of the lake is now dry; MONO LAKE, 1962: The tops of the two tufa towers are barely visible above the lake's surface (photograph by Eben McMillan, courtesy Mono Lake Committee)

Bottom. MONO LAKE, 1968: The same tufa towers entirely exposed (courtesy Mono Lake Committee)

Right. MONO LAKE, 1982: The tufa towers high and dry; between 1941 and 1981, the lake fell forty-five vertical feet and doubled in salinity (courtesy Mono Lake Committee)

KELP, CHINA COVE, POINT LOBOS, 1940 (photograph by Edward Weston, courtesy Center for Creative Photography, © 1981 Arizona Board of Regents)

Opposite. WILLARD POND, an Audubon Society loon preserve near Hancock, New Hampshire, 1989 (photograph by Sally Gall, courtesy Lieberman & Saul Gallery, New York)

CHAPTER

6

HIGHWAYS
AND BYWAYS

Americans are constantly on the move. Faith in this singularly American freedom is clearly inherent in the national spirit and has motivated the commitment of resources to transportation on a vast scale. However, in the search for speed and convenience, America has abandoned rather than refined existing technologies in favor of new inventions, that has ultimately lead to the current state of national gridlock.

Since the early nineteenth century, America has changed its basic transportation system four times, with each change involving massive construction to create the infrastructure for barges, railroads, automobiles, and airplanes. Just as engineers finished digging an extensive network of canals, the canals were forsaken in favor of railroads and trolleys. When long-distance automotive travel became viable, the nation poured its resources into the interstate highway system. Jet airplanes easily outpaced trains and cars, and by the late 1960s, cities were linked by air, bringing an end to the era of transcontinental rail passenger service and relegating most highway travel to relatively short-distance passenger traffic. Americans look back longingly at their railroads, now widely regarded as the most refined mode of travel.

By 1890, just over twenty years after the meeting of the transcontinental rails at Promontory Point, Utah, four routes stretched across the United States, and George Pullman had invented deluxe rail travel by introducing the first sleeping cars, by day convertible into parlors, saloons, or dining cars. At the turn of the century, in spite of the yen for interior luxury, the exteriors of American trains took on a distinctly rugged look, in keeping with the pioneering national self-image.

The Twentieth Century Limited, introduced in 1902 to provide overnight service

Opposite. Crews clearing the tracks of the Oregon Railway & Navigation Company from Rooster Rock to Oneonta Falls along the Columbia River to reach a passenger train stranded during the great winter storm of 1884–85; the passengers were ultimately rescued by riverboat (photograph by Carlton Emmons Watkins, courtesy Oregon Historical Society, negative ORHI 70143)

Page 112. The shallow-draft Mississippi steamboat, *J. G. Parke,* 1885 (photograph by Henry Bosse under the direction of Major Alexander Mackenzie, courtesy Sotheby's)

Page 113. A twenty-mule team hauls borax in Death Valley, California, circa 1900 (courtesy Nevada Historical Society, Reno)

between New York and Chicago, set the standard for luxury rail travel and was advertised as "The Greatest Train in the World." Luxury trains often had a compartment observation car, which featured three staterooms, a drawing room, library, buffet service, and a marvelous lounge with special windows from which one could view the scenery. The solarium lounge car provided an observation room appointed with armchairs, a separate smoking room, ladies' lounge, library, buffet service, and shower baths.

In the 1930s five trains ran daily from Chicago to California. By 1937 the Morning Daylight, racing over California flatland, had achieved a speed of eighty miles per hour. The first air-conditioned diner in the West was installed on the transcontinental Santa Fe Chief, popular with movie stars because it offered "roaming room" in the club car, as well as a barber and shower baths for men and women.

As late as the early 1960s the Broadway Limited was equipped with a telephone and offered a fine restaurant, complete with a headwaiter in tails; bar car; and overnight accommodations with private sitting rooms to which breakfast and a personalized weather forecast, printed en route, was delivered before arrival.

However, the 1970s saw the collapse of the Penn Central Line and a financial empire in tatters. Today, with modern jet travel and a highway system built at a cost of several trillion dollars, the remaining passenger railroads survive on government subsidies, deluxe air travel is a shadow of opulent railroad accommodations, and luxury automobiles have become the primary means of first-class travel.

America's automotive society worked well for more than three decades until the concept of a nation paved with highways backfired and the notion of a "freeway" took on a pithy irony. Ultimately, many people stopped walking, leading to

The passengers of a White Steamer Model E encountered convicts in prison stripes building a highway on February 2, 1906, while touring Florida after the Ormond-Daytona Races (photograph by Nick Lazarnick, courtesy National Automotive History Collection, Detroit Public Library, Lazarnick Collection)

Top. MARKET STREET, BETWEEN 15TH AND 16TH STREETS, DENVER, COLORADO, 1865 (photographer unknown, courtesy Collection Centre Canadien d'Architecture/Canadian Center for Architecture, Montreal)

Bottom. MAIN STREET OF COUNTY SEAT, ALABAMA, 1936 (photograph by Walker Evans, courtesy Library of Congress)

large numbers of pudgy suburbanites who drive from supermarket to drugstore, circling shopping malls like a tribe of Indians trying to purchase the covered wagons.

Los Angeles has become so choked with cars, that the Federal guidelines for ozone, the chief factor in the creation of smog, are exceeded on average 137.5 days per year. In the late 1980s BMW began running advertisements describing its vehicles as the most satisfying in which to endure a Los Angeles traffic jam. The cellular car telephone came to the rescue, but soon, it too was gridlocked.

The nightmare of gridlock pales by the sight of the decay of the urban road system which has become most visible in stalled traffic. There are few more gruesome stretches than the road from the airport to the downtown of almost any American city. Inevitably, the traveler is greeted by a crumbling highway, lined with heaps of refuse. Efforts at repair confound the motorist, snarling traffic in the summer when recreational travel is at its peak.

Although at first a status symbol reserved for the wealthy, automobiles were in widespread use before World War I. Like the railroads, the Model T represented the American "can-do" ideal during the first part of the twentieth century. Viewed romantically today, trains and early automobiles were, perhaps, the last technological advances whose inner workings were widely understood. However, nostalgia buffs who bemoan the demise of the grand days of luxury travel should ponder what one well-heeled lady said upon arrival in Hyannisport, "There are two ways to travel: first class and with children."

ORE TRACKS, NEAR SANTA CRUZ, CALIFORNIA
(photograph by Edward L. Woods, circa 1904,
courtesy The J. Paul Getty Museum, salt print,
11⁷/₁₆″ × 8¹¹/₁₆″)

Opposite. This runaway locomotive burst
through the wall of a Hartford roundhouse on
Saturday, July 8, 1905 (courtesy Connecticut Historical Society, Hartford, Connecticut)

Ocean Beach, San Francisco, circa 1930 (courtesy San Francisco Public Library)

Opposite. An automobile travels down the one-lane, oil-surfaced highway to Palm Springs in 1921; with shoulders of soft sand, passing had to be done with great care (photograph by Humphrey Birge from the collection of Caroline Birge Summers, courtesy Palm Springs Historical Society)

Page 122. STORM, Arizona, 1941 (photograph by Edward Weston, © 1981 Arizona Board of Regents, Center for Creative Photography)

Page 123. THE ROAD WEST, New Mexico, 1938 (photograph by Dorothea Lange, courtesy Houk Friedman Gallery, New York)

Ribbons of highways form CHICAGO LANDSCAPE NUMBER 117, 1966 (photograph by Art Sinsabaugh, courtesy Indiana University Art Museum)

New York's Third Avenue El after a snowstorm, 1942 (photograph by Josef Breitenbach, courtesy Hirschl & Adler Modern, New York)

Page 126. A country road near Keota in northeast Colorado vanishes with a dip in the plains (photograph by Robert Adams, 1973, courtesy Fraenkel Gallery, San Francisco)

Page 127. WEST OF HAVRE, MONTANA, 1968 (photograph © David Plowden, courtesy Catherine Edelman Gallery, Chicago)

Page 128. FREEWAY RAIN, Interstate 215, San Bernardino, California, 1976 (photograph by Roger Minick)

Page 129. ONTARIO INTERCHANGE at the intersection of Interstate 10 and Interstate 15, Ontario, California, 1976 (photograph by Roger Minick)

THE INDUSTRIAL LANDSCAPE

Describing the scope of the American industrial landscape is something like depicting an aging bull. One starts with the details, such as the horns, ears, and tail, but the enormity of the industrial beast is not apparent until one looks at the environmental havoc it has wrought. Yet, its economic muscle is what keeps America prosperous.

Until the 1960s the industrial landscape was largely regarded with pride. Renowned painter and photographer Charles Sheeler made a series of photographs at the Ford Motor Company's River Rouge plant in Dearborn, Michigan, in 1927, just before the Model A was introduced. His photographs glorified the values of the machine age and its products. However, those same values ultimately led to the blanket of smog now hovering over America's cities.

The fate of a city often hinges on its industy. Since its inception in the first part of the nineteenth century Lowell, Massachusetts, has traveled the full economic circle. Named for Francis Cabot Lowell, a Boston merchant who toured British textile mills and adapted their innovative designs for water-powered machinery, the city was founded by a group of Lowell's friends shortly after his death. They acquired a site for the new city by a waterfall in the Merrimack River and dug canals to harness waterpower for the mills. Lowell was a great success, and by 1840 it was the largest manufacturing center in America.

However, as electric power came to supplant waterpower, manufacturing centers spread west and south across America, and Lowell entered a period of spiraling decline that lasted for almost a century. Not until the late 1970s, with the introduction of high-technology industries, did prosperity return to Lowell. Vacant nineteenth-century brick factory buildings were rejuvenated to house high-technology companies that sprang up with the success of Wang and other corpo-

In 1901 Captain Anthony F. Lucas brought in the world's greatest gusher at Spindletop that led the oil stampede to Texas (photograph by Trost, courtesy The Texas Mid-Continent Oil & Gas Association, Austin)

Opposite. Smoke darkens the sky in Seattle, Washington, circa 1905 (courtesy Special Collections Division, University of Washington Libraries, negative UW 349)

Page 130. Big Lake Oil Company camp town, Texon, Texas, at the well site of Santa Rita No. 1, looking west from the top of Derrick No. 9, July 29, 1928 (photograph by E. J. Banks, courtesy The Petroleum Museum, Lilla Beyer Carter Collection)

Page 131. FIRE IN AMES MILLS, Oswego, New York, 1853 (daguerreotype with applied color, courtesy International Museum of Photography at George Eastman House)

SITE OF THE GOULD AND CURRY MINE, Virginia City, Nevada, 1979; this photograph was taken from the same vantage point as the one on the left, 111 years later (photograph by Mark Klett for the Rephotographic Survey Project)

Opposite. QUARTZ MILL, NEAR VIRGINIA CITY, Nevada, 1868 (photograph by Timothy O'Sullivan, courtesy United States Geological Survey)

rations that manufactured mid-size computers. On the strength of a single industry, Lowell was reborn and came to symbolize the Massachusetts miracle. However, with the introduction of versatile personal computers and work stations, the market for mid-size computers imploded, and Lowell's economic miracle again lay in ashes. Magnificent factory buildings again stand vacant, waiting hopefully for a fresh round of tenants.

Today an oil spill is regarded as a ghastly mess, but in the machine age an oil gusher was synonymous with great good fortune. The world's greatest gusher was brought in at the Spindletop Field in East Texas in 1901, when Captain Anthony Lukas struck oil at just over a thousand feet. For nine days crude oil roared into the sky at the rate of 100,000 barrels per day. In 1904 in northern Santa Barbara County, Union Oil's Hartnell Number 1, known as "Old Maud," gushed 12,000 barrels per day. Oil ran down the creeks and gullies of the California hillside. When a valve was closed to halt the flow, miniature geysers of oil sprouted through gopher holes and other divots in the surrounding fields.

East Texas and Santa Barbara were perceived as local problems. However, in 1969, as Americans watched in horror as an oil slick the depth of an inch crept inexorably toward Santa Barbara's pristine white beaches, pollution became a national issue. When a portion of the petrochemically saturated Cuyahoga River, which flows through the midst of Cleveland, caught on fire later that year for the third time in two decades, an outraged public believed that it had seen enough and thought it was high time for environmental action. Little did they know that the nuclear nightmare was on the horizon.

The most haunting image of industrial America was provided by the black and white surveillance cameras at the Three Mile Island nuclear power plant in 1979, when it suffered a partial core meltdown due to a loss of coolant. Millions of Americans wondered if all was lost and where they could flee. Fortunately, radiation from the first televised nuclear disaster was largely contained, but the second such major incident, the horror of Chernobyl in the Soviet Union in 1986, clearly answered the question: "What happens when a nuclear power plant goes out of control?"

Since building the bomb that leveled Nagasaki, the nuclear-weapons plant in Hanford, Washington, has been oozing radiation. In 1972 the Atomic Energy Commission discovered that the underground storage tanks at Hanford, which hold millions of gallons of the most lethal radioactive wastes, were leaking on a massive scale, and that one tank had already lost 115,000 gallons of liquid nuclear waste. Hundreds of miles downstream, shellfish in the Columbia River became radioactive from Hanford's routine radiation dumping. In one ten-year period the quantity of radioactive iodine released into the atmosphere at Hanford rivaled that of Chernobyl. Some area residents have been exposed to a 3,000-rad dose of radioactive

Panorama of the Ajo open copper mining pit operations in Arizona, May 1934 (courtesy Phelps Dodge Corporation)

iodine to their thyroids—six hundred times the maximum allowable annual rate for federal workers.

Radiation knows no boundaries. Fugitive plutonium from the notorious Rocky Flats Nuclear Weapons Plant in Colorado has so contaminated the land to the west of Denver that developers have been forbidden to build there. When the plant was finally closed in 1989, the government commissioned a study to determine whether radiation could have reached poisonous levels in downtown Denver.

However, a savior is on the horizon. The dream of solar power has become a reality on 1,300 acres of California's Mojave Desert. Eight solar thermal plants operated by Luz International use curved mirrors to track the sun, amplifying its heat eighty times, to spin steam turbines that generate pollution-free electricity for 385,000 southern California homes.

These plants provide maximum power during sultry summer days when it is most needed and pollution is at its worst. At night and on cloudy days the boilers run on natural gas. A fully operational solar thermal plant releases into the atmosphere 85 percent less nitrogen oxide and 75 percent less carbon dioxide than a

conventional gas-fired plant.

The generation of solar power involves about the same amount of land as conventional power sources, which require the mining, refining, and distribution of fossil fuels. To protect endangered species such as the desert tortoise, the Barstow woolly sunflower, and the Mojave ground squirrel, Luz International sets aside five acres of desert land as a state-run conservancy for every pristine acre utilized by its power plants.

But no one really knows what to do about the various kinds of lethal waste. American industry has run out of land for its disposal and a reprocessing plant is rarely regarded as a neighborhood asset. Industrial and legislative oil and gas interests have combined in an attempt to foil the further development of clean solar power. In 1990 the federal government announced that the same companies that created the mountains of nuclear waste would be retained to clean it up. This program is not unlike converting concentration-camp guards into doctors and nurses to care for the surviving inmates.

The American public, frustrated by the numbing litany of industrial catastrophes and the accompanying lack of corporate accountability, remains fully aware that industry is the engine that powers the economy. Yet, only the most delicate balancing of interests will permit the coexistence of a prosperous economy and a clean environment in which to enjoy the fruits of the industrial landscape.

The tensular strength and grace of the steel industry was the subject of ARMCO STEEL, Ohio, 1922 (photograph by Edward Weston, © 1981 Arizona Board of Regents, Center for Creative Photography)

Opposite. BIRMINGHAM STEEL MILL AND WORKERS' HOUSES, 1936 (photograph by Walker Evans, courtesy Library of Congress)

MANHATTAN AND THE EAST RIVER, NEW YORK CITY, 1931 (photograph by Samuel H. Gottscho, courtesy Collection Centre Canadien d'Architecture/ Canadian Center for Architecture, Montreal)

Opposite. PITTSBURGH, 1941 (photograph by Edward Weston, courtesy The J. Paul Getty museum, silver gelatin print, 7⁹⁄₁₆″ × 9½″, © 1981 Arizona Board of Regents, Center for Creative Photography)

Page 142. Cleveland's Cuyahoga River on fire, November 3, 1952 (photograph by James Thomas, courtesy *The Cleveland Press* Collection/ Cleveland State University Archives)

Page 143. Crude oil splattered the Santa Barbara coastline in the aftermath of the 1969 spill (courtesy Department of Special Collections, UCSB Library)

Page 144. Hazardous waste site at the TOOELE ARMY DEPOT (NORTH AREA), TOOELE, UTAH (detail), May 1986, from the series *Waste Land*, 1985–88 (photograph by David T. Hanson; detail; original in color)

Page 145. COOLING TOWER, NUCLEAR GENERATING PLANT, STILLMAN VALLEY, ILLINOIS, 1981 (photograph © David Plowden, courtesy Catherine Edelman Gallery, Chicago)

CHAPTER

8

SPRAWL

Levittown started it all. Construction began with the baby boom after World War II on a tract of potato farms in Hempstead, Long Island. More than seventeen thousand identical homes were laid out in the pattern of swirling subdivisions. Critics condemned the project as sterile and were astonished when families flocked to live there. What were once thought to be minuscule lots are now considered spacious enough to hold a second home. It's hard to find a house that hasn't been modified. The saplings have grown into mature, graceful trees.

After Levittown came the deluge. Development spread across America like a lava flow, engulfing everything in its path. Children of the fifties may remember picking apples and raspberries at their grandparents' farms. As teenagers, they watched their neighbors' land sprout gas stations and supermarkets. By the time they graduated from college, their grandparents' fields had become parking lots for regional shopping malls.

Malls revolutionized the way Americans live. Traditionally, development had gathered around sources of energy and transportation, such as harbors or railroads. When the first malls were inserted into the landscape, seemingly at random, entirely new patterns of employment were created. The malls, rather than harbors, rivers, or highways, formed the hub around which residential development spread.

As the shopping center evolved from the early squat cinder-block construction of the late 1950s, America's downtowns began to crumble and decay. Once-gracious buildings with vaulted ceilings were either torn down and rebuilt in the image of the glass box or left to slowly wither and die. Parks were let go. Violent crime became rampant. The new malls featured safety, convenience, and controlled environments. As private property the homeless could be kept out and the soap box

Main road into Newport shortly before the turn of the century (© John T. Hoph, from *Newport Then & Now*)

Page 147. COOPERSTOWN, LOOKING EAST FROM HANNAH'S HILL, circa 1865 (Smith-Telfer Photographic Collection, courtesy New York State Historical Association, Cooperstown)

The same road, circa 1980 (© John T. Hoph, from *Newport Then & Now*)

Page 150. SAN DIEGO, CALIFORNIA, circa 1870–75 (photograph by Carlton Emmons Watkins, courtesy The J. Paul Getty Museum, detail of an albumen print, 4″ × 6¹/₁₆″)

Page 151. The same view of San Diego, but from a highter vantage point, 1990 (photograph by P. M. Bowers)

pulled out from beneath the feet of the nagging problems created by freedom of speech. New mall architecture arrived with open interiors and amenities, such as theaters, restaurants, and cultural events, creating a sad parody of the life that once graced the forgotten downtowns.

Suburban towns such as Stamford, Connecticut, became cities in their own right and were quickly overwhelmed by the big-city problems of overcrowding, crime, and high taxes. San Diego stands out in sharp contrast. In 1985 the Hann Company opened Horton Plaza, a new mall that covers almost seven downtown blocks with shopping, dining, and entertainment facilities. With a postmodern exterior designed to reflect the existing buildings, Horton Plaza has become San Diego's third largest tourist attraction and now functions in ways similar to the great downtowns of the past.

In 1967 the Rouse Corporation broke ground to create the entirely new town of Columbia, Maryland, situated within commuting distance of Washington and Baltimore. Approximately 73,000 people now live in over 27,500 residential units. A typical house is sited on an open field or a wooded lot of about one-third of an acre. The subdivisions are laid out to minimize the impact of automobile traffic, resulting in quiet neighborhoods where children can walk to school. Over 2,300 acres are set aside for parks, playgrounds, and natural areas, in addition to the broad array of commercial, recreational, educational, and cultural facilities. The design worked.

However, development devours an incredible amount of land. The rule of thumb in designing a shopping-mall parking lot is five parking spaces for every thousand square feet of commercial space. No residential development is complete without

a patchwork of lawns. As of 1987 Americans had planted more than 25 million acres of lawn, an area about the size of Indiana.

Developers and environmentalists are on a collision course and water is the battleground. In 1988, with burgeoning residential construction in the watershed area for New York City's reservoirs in the Catskill Mountains—an area roughly the size of Delaware—doctors advised individuals with low salt tolerances to avoid city water because the rock salt used by road crews to clear snow was leaching into the reservoirs. In 1991 New York began enforcing nearly century-old laws restricting development to avoid massive expenditures for filtering its water. The pace of new construction in coastal Rhode Island has slowed to a crawl because much of the land fails the new strict percolation tests. All of Long Island's drinking water comes from an underground lake of finite supply, highly vulnerable to contamination. In 1990 developments in the pine barrens of Suffolk County were halted by court order. Water rationing has become a fact of life on the central coast of California. Gone is the era when water shortages could be solved by building another dam or aqueduct.

An alternative has been to go where water is plentiful and real estate relatively inexpensive. In the 1980s the nearly completed network of interstate highways set off an unprecedented real-estate boom in commuter homes and second homes. As the pace of transportation has accelerated, the distances between the home and workplace and the home and weekend house have vastly expanded. Tiny, obscure towns in the Maine woods have become part of the weekend belt around Boston because they are two hundred fifty miles away or just under a five-hour drive.

Top. An arch over Freemont Street, probably installed to celebrate the dedication of Boulder Dam, known today as Hoover Dam, welcomes visitors to Las Vegas, circa 1935 (courtesy Alicia Lawrence Collection, University of Nevada, Las Vegas Library, Special Collections)

Bottom. Today Las Vegas comes alive at night, and visitors are greeted by a glittering light show (courtesy Las Vegas News Bureau)

Before the automobile, the highway, and large-scale development, the front yard was set aside for social experiences, such as greeting a neighbor out for an evening stroll or friends riding by in a horse-drawn carriage. When cars began anonymously whizzing by, homeowners sought refuge in the privacy and solitude of their back yards where the laundry used to hang before the era of modern appliances. The front yard was left to show off the house, known in real-estate vernacular as "curb appeal."

Property values have become paramount. By planting a single large tree, home-owners have found that they can increase the value of their houses by 10 percent. Cutting down trees can reduce a property's value by 20 to 30 percent. Many communities have adopted laws limiting lawn height to four inches on the theory that shaggy lawns adversely affect a neighborhood's property values.

By the late 1980s urban and suburban sprawl had become interchangeable, and a growing consensus concluded that the American landscape had gone out of balance. Suddenly, New Jersey, the quintessential home of suburban cookie-cutter architecture, wants to be the Garden State again. But America still needs to build 2 million housing units a year to house its expanding population. Circumstances may alter the pace and style of construction, but they won't halt it. Real-estate development is as American as rock and roll. As one developer put it: "I love the smell of charbroiled steaks in the evening. It smells like . . . the suburbs."

MILLWORKERS' HOUSES IN WILLIMANTIC, CONNECTI-CUT, 1931 (photograph by Walker Evans, courtesy The J. Paul Getty Museum, silver gelatin print, 5¹¹/₁₆″ × 7³/₈″)

Opposite. The delicate beauty and harmony of a single clapboard house in a wooded landscape is conveyed by EQUIVALENT, MUSIC NUMBER 1, LAKE GEORGE, 1922 (photograph by Alfred Stieglitz, courtesy The J. Paul Getty Museum, platinum print, 9⅝″ × 12⁷/₁₆″, 87. ×M 94.4)

Page 154. GREEN RIVER BUTTES, GREEN RIVER, WYO-MING, 1872 (photograph by Timothy O'Sullivan, courtesy United States Geological Survey)

Page 155. Castle Rock, GREEN RIVER, WYOMING, 1979; this photograph was taken from the same vantage point as the one on the left, 107 years later (photograph by Mark Klett and Gordon Bushaw for the Rephotographic Survey Project)

RENTAL CABINS, NEAR WOODSTOCK, NEW HAMP-SHIRE, 1935; was originally titled LIKE DOLLS' HOUSES (photograph by Frank Navara, courtesy Collection Centre Canadien d'Architecture/ Canadian Center for Architecture, Montreal)

Opposite. CHICAGO LANDSCAPE NUMBER 308, 1967 (photograph by Art Sinsabaugh, courtesy Indiana University Art Museum)

Page 160. In 1976 land was graded in preparation for the construction of the Las Colinas Urban Center in Dallas (photograph by Landiscor Aerial Photo, courtesy Goldman Sachs & Co.)

Page 161. Ten years later the office buildings at the Las Colinas Urban Center were completed, and a man-made lake lapped at their shores, 1986 (photograph by Landiscor Aerial Photo, courtesy Goldman Sachs & Co.)

Rolling out an instant sod lawn in Livermore, southern California, circa 1970 (photograph by Bill Owens, from *Suburbia*)

Opposite. Roof and parking lot of a sorority house at the University of Mississippi, Oxford, 1981 (photograph by Alen MacWeeney)

Page 162. AFTERMATH: THE WICHITA FALLS, TEXAS, TORNADO NUMBER 14A–4503, MCNEILL ROAD, LOOKING NORTH, APRIL 14, 1979 (photograph by Frank Gohlke, from a series of twenty, courtesy Franklin Parrasch Gallery, New York, and Bonnie Benrubi Fine Arts, New York)

Page 163. AFTERMATH, NUMBER 14B–4503, MCNEILL ROAD, LOOKING NORTH, JUNE 1980, Wichita Falls, Texas (photograph by Frank Gohlke, from a series of twenty, courtesy Franklin Parrasch Gallery, New York, and Bonnie Benrubi Fine Arts, New York)

CHAPTER

9

SKYLINES

Few sights can match the New York City skyline seen from the harbor as the lights come on in the afterglow of the sunset. The city seems clean, almost rational. Alfred Stieglitz called his 1910 picture of the New York skyline *The City of Ambition*. The skyline has evolved, but the spirit of ambition remains. Today, the buildings are corporate rather than personal monuments, reflecting the boardroom mentality that overtook American business in the intervening years.

The history of New York's architecture is one of constant evolution and expansion caused in part by the steadily rising urban population. In the early nineteenth century grand residential neighborhoods rose from the fields and pastures to house the wealthy. The lofty spires of new stone churches pierced the sky. During the 1840s St. John's Park was described as ''a spot of Eden loveliness and exclusiveness.''

Unfortunately, much of what was so grandly designed and properly constructed has now been torn down. St. John's Park was plowed under by Cornelius Vanderbilt for a railroad depot that now is an entrance ramp to the Holland Tunnel. Only vestiges of earlier days, such as Greenwich Village and Chelsea, remain. Gramercy Park, owned by the tenants of the surrounding buildings, who must unanimously agree on any change, is still believed safe from demolition.

However, the most dramatic change to a skyline always occurs with sudden disaster, and New York's architectural growing pains appear trivial when contrasted with the catastrophic fires that leveled three of America's greatest cities: Chicago, Boston, and San Francisco. Each city was destroyed during a period of national optimism, only to rise like the Phoenix from the ashes of its foundations.

Viewing the ruins as an architectural opportunity, the citizens of Chicago, Boston,

Page 166. FRANKLYN STREET, LOOKING DOWN, Boston, Massachusetts, circa 1860 (photograph by John P. Soule, courtesy The Boston Athenaeum)

Page 167. THE GREAT FIRE OF BOSTON, ON PERKINS STREET AND PEARL STREET, LOOKING TO BROAD, 1872 (photograph by James Wallace Black, courtesy The J. Paul Getty Museum, albumen print, 7¹¹/₁₆" x 7 ⁷/₁₆")

RUINS OF THE GREAT FIRE, Boston's Burnt District,
circa 1872 (photograph by David W. Butterfield,
courtesy The Boston Athenaeum)

and San Francisco worked from scratch to reconstruct their cities "bigger, better than ever." The motivation for their intense determination to rebuild lies in part with what they were forced to witness as the flames capriciously consumed the cities in which they lived.

Chicago was originally built in the span of a generation. It had risen from marshland to become a prosperous city of three hundred thousand inhabitants who dreamed of becoming the commercial and cultural center of America. But on Sunday evening, October 8, 1871, everything went wrong.

According to legend, as Mrs. O'Leary milked her cow in her barn on the north side of De Koven Street, the cow kicked a kerosene lantern into the hay. The hay, dry as kindling from a rainless summer, burst into flames and the fire spread quickly as the southwest wind fanned the flames north to the heart of the city.

The frame houses and shanties of Chicago's West Side were the first to go. At Van Buren Street the fire vaulted the Chicago River. Then at one o'clock in the morning the Chamber of Commerce collapsed followed by the Court House two hours later. Like the band playing as the Titanic went down, its great bell tolled to the end.

An ocean of flames, surging in mile-long waves, coiled around the entire commercial district creating a spectacular red and orange inferno. Nothing was overlooked. Sherman House, Palmer House, the Opera House, the Grand Pacific Hotel, even cemetery markers, were consumed before the fire reached Lake Michigan and had nowhere left to go.

The north side of De Koven Street was in ashes, but along with other dwellings on the south side of the street, Mrs. O'Leary's house survived. A newspaper

Palmer House before the 1871 Chicago fire (courtesy The Chicago Public Library, Special Collections, negative CCW 5.39)

Palmer House after the 1871 Chicago fire (courtesy The Chicago Public Library, Special Collections, negative CCW 5.40)

reporter observed, "I found De Koven Street at last, a mean little street of shabby wooden houses . . . falling to decay. The street, unpaved and littered with old boxes and mildewed papers, and a dozen absurd geese wandering around with rustic familiarity . . . had no look of Chicago about it."

Rival cities could barely conceal their grinning satisfaction. A New Orleans newspaper wrote, "Chicago will not be like the Carthage of old. Its glory will be of the past . . . while its hopes, once so bright and cloudless, will be to the end marred and blackened by the smoke of its fiery fate." After the fire Chicago's greatest promoter, John Steven Wright, walked down the charred, smoldering ruins of Wabash Avenue. Mocked by remarks about Chicago's future, he replied, "Chicago will have more men, more money, more business within five years than she would have had without the fire." A day later John McKnight's fruit and cider stand was operating amid the rubble of Clark Street. Within a week more than five thousand temporary structures had been erected and two hundred buildings were under construction.

It was a bonanza for architects, who replaced the downtown with taller buildings that foreshadowed the skyscraper. Salt was added to cure cement so bricks could be laid in winter. When electric lights were available, construction continued into the night. A British visitor noted that during most of 1872 "there was built and completed . . . a brick, stone, or iron warehouse every hour of every working day."

Thirteen months and a day later, on Saturday November 9, 1872, the Great Boston Fire ruined another weekend. Around seven o'clock in the evening a dry-goods store on the corner of Summer and Kingston streets burst into flames. With water pressure too weak and hoses too short, the firemen were unable to direct enough water to reach the mansard roof of the five-story structure.

Sparks and flames jumped from roof to roof and shot across the narrow street, igniting stores and warehouses, which were packed with dry, flammable goods that burned like torches in the night. As the fire spread, elegant granite and marble façades crumbled with the intense heat and collapsed in the street. Around midnight a gas explosion reignited Summer Street, and only a heroic effort to save the Old South Meeting House halted the flames at Milk Street. When the fire was finally contained about lunchtime on Sunday, the tenth, more than a thousand buildings covering nearly seventy acres had been leveled. The leather and dry-goods industries were completely obliterated, as were most of the publishers and printers.

Photographs of The Burnt District were in immediate demand, especially those by the renowned photographers Whipple and Black, whose studio was across the street from where the fire had stopped. In December James Black complained that "for the past week I have had hardly time to take a breath, such has been the call for photographs of The Burnt District."

Although a disaster of staggering proportions, the fire was regarded by Bostonians as a temporary paralysis, like a weekend blizzard. Just as a heavy snowfall is cleared by Monday morning, signs were erected in the debris, directing customers to temporary offices. Architect Nathaniel J. Bradlee wrote in his diary that because of the fire he had received fourteen commissions for new buildings. The ruins were leveled, the streets were widened, and a rejuvenated commercial district arose from the ashes.

San Francisco met its first demise at 5:13 A.M. on the morning of April 18, 1906,

This 1860 photograph of Boston was taken from a hot-air balloon, tethered to the Boston Common, that hovered over an area of the city that was later destroyed in the great Boston fire; surprisingly, wind was not the major problem confronting the photographer, but rather the intense heat generated by the balloon, which upset the delicate balance of his plates and chemicals (photograph by James Wallace Black, courtesy The Bostonian Society)

Opposite. VIEW OF BOSTON FROM COMMERCIAL WHARF, 1975 (photograph by Nicholas Nixon, courtesy Zabriskie Gallery, New York)

with a long, grinding rumble as the San Andreas fault shuddered for forty-eight seconds and then, with a final jarring convulsion, shifted back into place. The roar of crashing glass, china, chimneys, and the splintering of wood was accompanied by the howls of moaning cattle near the waterfront. Then silence; absolute quiet. The air was choked with dust and smoke, a harbinger of the fires was still to come.

No fire alarm ever sounded. From Nob Hill the damage appeared to be contained, except for the thick column of smoke rising ominously from the area south of Market Street. Upon close inspection, a desperate battle was under way to rescue the buried and control the blaze. Without water, the results were pitiful. Caruso had charmed fashionable San Francisco the night before. By nine in the morning the Grand Opera House had been reduced to cinders.

The scope of the fire was beyond experience or imagination. As the flames crept uptown toward the ruins of City Hall, the injured in the nearby Mechanics Pavilion were evacuated, but not for the last time. Residents faced with the inevitable incineration of their homes hauled their possessions to the homes of friends only to watch them burn a few hours later. At 11:00 A.M. the eighteen-story Call Building went up like a torch in a shower of falling glass, and at 3:00 P.M. San Francisco's heart was broken as flames roared through the Palm Court of the beloved Palace Hotel. Burning hopelessly out of control, San Francisco was a city in retreat. Residents headed for the Panhandle, the Presidio, Twin Peaks, and Golden Gate Park. No sanctuary was too far away.

A. P. Giannini, a banker disguised as a fruit seller, directed through the crowd a horse-drawn cart piled high with orange crates under which was concealed eighty thousand dollars in gold, the entire cash reserve of San Francisco's Bank of Italy.

MAIN AND SPRING STREETS, LOS ANGELES, CALIFORNIA, circa 1870–75 (photograph by Carlton Emmons Watkins, courtesy The J. Paul Getty Museum, albumen print, 4″ x 6″)

Giannini proceeded without interference to his San Mateo home, where he stashed the gold in the living room fireplace. With the rescued gold he helped rebuild the city.

By two o'clock Thursday morning all four sides of Union Square and the St. Francis Hotel were ablaze. Then Chinatown fell. At 4:30 A.M. soldiers began removing the paintings from the Huntington mansion and the Mark Hopkins house on Nob Hill. California Street was piled high with Renoirs, Monets, and Flemish tapestries from the Crocker house. By 11:00 A.M. Nob Hill was gone, and with it the unfinished, brilliant white Fairmont Hotel.

While the wealthy fled San Francisco in automobiles, fire fighters, soldiers, and volunteers made a final stand at Van Ness Avenue. Fire hoses drawing salt water from the Bay were run more than a mile up the avenue. At noon a man climbed the steeple of St. Mary's Cathedral to beat out the flames. Miraculously, at 6:00 P.M. a working hydrant was found. The struggle was intensely physical. Fire fighters ripped burning shingles off the smoldering buildings with their bare hands.

At 3:00 A.M. Friday morning the wind shifted, blowing the flames back toward

A panoramic view of lower Manhattan in 1876 from the Brooklyn tower of the Brooklyn Bridge, prior to placing the suspension cables, 1876 (photograph by J. H. Beale, courtesy The New York Historical Society, New York City)

the Bay. The fire line at Van Ness had held, but at the cost of Telegraph Hill. By nightfall, as the fireboats doused the last remnants of the blaze, the United States Mint was still standing along with a whiskey warehouse. Other structures stood through the devastation at unpredictable intervals. However, twenty-five thousand buildings, including the city's cultural and commercial heart, had been reduced to ashes, and almost a quarter of a million people were without shelter.

The San Francisco the world knew had gone up in smoke. The nation rushed to help, but President Roosevelt declined offers of foreign aid. The United States could take care of its own and build a new city, even though the earth shook beneath its foundations. Soon the air in San Francisco was electric with excitement as the city planners began the grand design of "a metropolis finer than Paris."

No one talks about fixing things better than ever anymore. Unlike the first San Francisco earthquake, which gave the city a fresh start, the second, in 1989, left the city shattered, and the rebuilding has been a tedious, demoralizing process. Although the severed Bay Bridge was repaired in a matter of weeks, San Francisco's transportation system was still in disarray a year later. Repairs of all kinds moved

STEEL WORKERS ON TOP OF THE EMPIRE STATE BUILDING MOORING MAST, circa 1932 (photograph by Lewis Hine, courtesy Sotheby's)

Opposite. Group portrait of the men who paint the Brooklyn Bridge, October 7, 1914 (courtesy Municipal Archives, Department of Records and Information Services, City of New York)

at a snail's pace as bureaucrats pointed fingers at each other. The Phoenix has yet to rise again.

While Chicago, Boston, and San Francisco experienced the mixed blessing of starting over, other cities have mimicked New York's architectural passion for building and rebuilding—a passion that led to the construction of the universal corporate skyline. Gordon Bunshaft, the architect who died in 1990, was the father of the modern corporate glass and steel design that evolved from the International Style. His buildings on Park Avenue, such as Lever House, Union Carbide, Manufacturers Hanover, and Pepsi-Cola, were constructed during the 1950s in an era of corporate infallibility and reflected cool, corporate modernism. But the contemporary success of these buildings has led to a deluge of corporate structures that has created an architectural blight.

America believed that it could build its way out of the crisis of urban social decay and committed resources on an unparalleled scale to do so. By the end of the 1970s almost every city had a new skyline, and had begun to look like every other city. At night urban problems were masked by the clean fluorescent glow emanating from the forests of corporate towers constructed to house lawyers and investment bankers. In Hartford, Connecticut, the gold dome of the state capitol crowns an island of insurance towers ringed by poverty.

During the 1980s the city of Hartford offered financial incentives for corporations to relocate their headquarters in proximity to New York and Boston. Hundreds of millions of dollars poured into the city, office space tripled, and a glittering glass skyline rose. Developers warehoused entire vacant blocks of downtown, waiting for the moment to turn them into glittering new office towers.

NEW YORK CITY FROM THE EMPIRE STATE BUILDING UNDER CONSTRUCTION, 1931 (photograph by Lewis Hine, courtesy Sotheby's)

As Hartford's development engine seized, all the problems of an aging urban center resurfaced, shattering the concept that shimmering new façades could transcend municipal blight. Hotels, including the 410-room Hilton, went out of business along with the Sage-Allen department store, a fixture on Main Street for 101 years.

Too many towers were built too fast. Little time was available for architectural evolution, and developers were reluctant to pay for innovation. During the era of corporate deification, corporate towers were often described as modern-day church spires. In the post–junk-bond era darkened office towers have taken on the look of grotesque tombstones.

Many corporate towers have not aged gracefully. What were vital, fresh ideas in the fifties often seem static in the nineties. Pride of ownership has proved elusive, as many corporations no longer own the buildings that bear their names. Bunshaft's Pepsi-Cola Building has changed hands several times. Even Mies van der Rohe's Seagram Building, the centerpiece of corporate Park Avenue, does not belong to Seagram anymore.

City dwellers seeking an end to the demolition-derby mentality of urban development have sought out remnants of America's national heritage. In New York the Landmarks Commission was formed to save what remained of pre–World War II architectural scale and harmony. Ironically, when a developer threatened to demolish Lever House the Landmarks Commission, fearing the worst, christened it a landmark as well. Fashions shifted. Preservation became the catchword of the nineties. Only time can measure the depth of the nation's cultural sincerity.

WABASH AVENUE AND WACKER DRIVE, CHICAGO, IL-LINOIS, circa 1930 (photograph by Langdon H. Longwell, courtesy Collection Centre Canadien d'Architecture/Canadian Center for Architecture, Montreal)

Opposite. RADIO CITY, NEW YORK, 1942 (photograph by Josef Breitenbach, courtesy Hirschl & Adler Modern, New York)

The United States Army Air Corps cruising over the Manhattan skyline in the 1930s (courtesy Municipal Archives, Department of Records and Information Services, City of New York)

Opposite. SS NORMANDIE docking in New York harbor, June 3, 1935 (courtesy Municipal Archives, Department of Records and Information Services, City of New York)

CHRYSLER BUILDING CONSTRUCTION, NEW YORK, 1930 (photograph by Walker Evans, courtesy The J. Paul Getty Museum, gelatin silver print, 6³/₁₆″ x 4¹⁵/₁₆″)

Opposite. REFLECTION, OLD ST. LOUIS COUNTY COURTHOUSE, 1975 (photograph by William Clift from COURTHOUSE, a bicentennial project funded by Joseph E. Seagram & Sons)

Page 188. LOS ANGELES SKYLINE, 1976, viewed from Bunker Hill (photograph by Roger Minick)

Page 189. VIEW OF MIDTOWN FROM 48TH STREET, New York, 1975 (photograph by Nicholas Nixon, courtesy Zabriskie Gallery, New York)

INDEX

Design: J. C. Suarès

Picture Coordinator: Lisa S. Adelson

A C K N O W L E D G M E N T S

The author wishes to express his gratitude to J. C. Suarès, who first proposed this project over a bowl of pasta at Mimi's Ristorante, for yet another brilliant design; to Lisa Adelson whose tireless research led to the discovery of many of the photographs published for the first time in this book; to my three editors, John Thornton, Mary Hall Mayer, and Paul Aron whose undeviating enthusiasm and support for this project have been instrumental in its fruition; to Isolde C. Sauer, my production editor, who saw the book through to completion; to Lessley Davis, production manager, who supervised the film preparation at M E Aslett, the printing at Arcata Graphics/Halliday and the binding at Horowitz; to Kathy and Linda Gates who made the dummy; to Arthur Bullowa for more than a decade of friendship and advice; to Walter Lord for the Civil War bees and for all the good years; to my Father and Mother who taught me to see; to Aunt Fanny who trusted in me; to the following individuals and institutions: Oliver Reese, H. H. Bennett Studio Foundation; Sally Pierce, The Boston Athenaeum; Roy McJunkin, California Museum of Photography; Lori Ritchie and Syvelin Gronquist, University of California, Santa Barbara; Gilles Lessard, Canadian Center for Architecture; Terence Pitts and Dianne Nilsen, Center for Creative Photography; Galen Wilson, Chicago Public Library; Paige Savery, Connecticut Historical Society; Pari Stave, Equitable Archive; Weston Naef, Louise Stover, Andrea Hales, and Betsy Lewis, The J. Paul Getty Museum; Richard Menschel and Judith Kolata, Goldman Sachs & Co.; Nan Brewer, Indiana University Art Museum; Spencer Kennard, Kelsey Kennard; Julia Van Haaften and Jan Murray, The New York Public Library; Kathy War, University of Nevada; Susan Seyl, Oregon Historical Society; Sally McManus, Palm Springs Historical Society; Betty Orbeck, The Petroleum Museum; Nicholas Balich and Leslie Nielson, Phelps Dodge Corporation; Terry Toedtemeier, Portland Art Museum; Robert Whitcomb, David Gray, and Maureen Aldrich, *Providence Journal*; Stephen Elliott, Sachem Publishing Associates; Beth Gates-Warren, Denise Bethel, and Carrie Frizell, Sotheby's; John Bromley, Union Pacific Railroad; Teresa Roane, The Valentine Museum; and, especially, to my wife, Charlotte Frieze, whose love sustains me.

The 1883 opening of the Brooklyn Bridge, designed by John Roebling, was celebrated with a massive fireworks display; a triumph of design and engineering it was the world's first steel suspension bridge and united the island of Manhattan with Brooklyn; the towers were built on wooden piers that are still in place and in 1883 were second only in height to the spire of Trinity Church in lower Manhattan. (courtesy Lisa S. Adelson Collection)